TRACKS GO MAD

ANAGH V

Copyright © Anagh V
All Rights Reserved.

This book has been self-published with all reasonable efforts taken to make the material error-free by the author. No part of this book shall be used, reproduced in any manner whatsoever without written permission from the author, except in the case of brief quotations embodied in critical articles and reviews.

The Author of this book is solely responsible and liable for its content including but not limited to the views, representations, descriptions, statements, information, opinions and references ["Content"]. The Content of this book shall not constitute or be construed or deemed to reflect the opinion or expression of the Publisher or Editor. Neither the Publisher nor Editor endorse or approve the Content of this book or guarantee the reliability, accuracy or completeness of the Content published herein and do not make any representations or warranties of any kind, express or implied, including but not limited to the implied warranties of merchantability, fitness for a particular purpose. The Publisher and Editor shall not be liable whatsoever for any errors, omissions, whether such errors or omissions result from negligence, accident, or any other cause or claims for loss or damages of any kind, including without limitation, indirect or consequential loss or damage arising out of use, inability to use, or about the reliability, accuracy or sufficiency of the information contained in this book.

Made with ♥ on the Notion Press Platform
www.notionpress.com

Contents

CHAPTER I

Triggered

It was a great stone-built hall with vast space filled by chairs of one kind. At the end of the hall was an inclined table-top ground, and on the inclined ground were gathered great amount of people.

Among them was Mihira. She was so desperate to see how the program goes ahead. But the only disadvantage with her was that she couldn't stand a view with her height. She tried several times, to lift her ankle but it took few minutes for her to realize that it was not high enough to match the heights of the people ahead. She grunted and came back to her own position. She always watched functions from the front view and wanted to see how a function carries on from behind. She had thought this was one chance she could use, but it looked in vain.

She slithered back to the end of the crowd. From there, she could actually breathe. She took a glance at the empty hall, which was about to be filled that very evening. The hall was not literally empty though. At a corner of the hall was her brother, seated in a chair, all alone. She then decided to spend time with him since no adult cared to give her attention. Although she could walk down the stairs, she leaped down the stage and slowly walked towards her brother.

Viraj on the other hand, had his mind busy and irritated. He had his phone in his hand, with his ankle on his knee. There was no one by him, until the next second, when Mihira arrived.

"What are you doing, brother?" she asked with utmost innocence. Viraj nodded.

"What do you mean by that?" she asked, advancing forward. Yet, no reply. Then he burst into an eruption of whines and growls. Mihira knew something troubled him. She dared and peeked into his phone where she found a bunch of photos, of forests and one person in common in all of them. "What are these?" Mihira asked. Viraj caught his head and started typing something.

Mihira knew how to get a word out of him.

"I am going to the ice-cream point!" she said, loud enough for him to hear, "Come with me to get them!"

Viraj seemed as if he didn't care enough to hear it. "I'm going!" Mihira said again, and turned back. She started walking again, gazing at the crowded stage, shaking her head. She at last came to the ice-cream point, where a bald man was scooping up ice-creams. They were inserted in small cups, with a spoon in them. Mihira took one of them as the coldness penetrated through her hands. She put a spoon in her mouth and started thinking, recalling the photos her brother was looking at. She tried to guess who the boy in the photos was. At last, she came to a decision, when she turned back and found Viraj.

"Who was that boy in the pictures?" Mihira asked.

"Farhan" replied Viraj, scratching his head.

"Yes! I guessed him correctly! I won the bet, so give me the reward!" she burst out in excitement. "I didn't bet you on anything" said Viraj, confused. Mihira filled air in her cheeks in frustration, "At least I succeeded in getting you off of that chair"

They placed themselves in two chairs. "So what's the matter with your 'Farhan'?"

* * *

Yugank had his earpieces fixed to his ears. His head nodded in a rhythm. He held his phone in one of his hands.

"Don't let me go!" came a shrill voice from the phone. "I have done...what I had to do..." he sang with the voice. He was, for some time, a part of the voice and that mild piano which sounded like a small, kind boy's voice. Something gentle touched his shoulder. He turned his head reluctantly away from his phone, to the source of that touch. He found a small boy, maybe of Fourth standard, dressed in a school uniform.

The boy held his hand out and gently touched his shoulder again. Yugank took off one of his earpieces. All the sounds of the conductor screaming for tickets, the bus honking, the vehicles on the road honking too, and then the bus replying with a honk, their engines rumbling, entered Yugank's ear and it sounded uncomfortable to him. He raised his eyebrows at the boy. The boy looked up to him, "Sorry if I disturbed you" he smiled.

"You did indeed but I'll excuse you for that" said Yugank, smiling back, "How can I help you?"

"Can I sit here, please?" the boy asked.

"Yeah, sure" Yugank moved closer to the window and the boy settled beside him.

"Thank you" said the boy. Yugank grinned wide and fixed the earpiece back to its place.

The song continued playing. The sounds from outside sounded so low now and he felt like he were back in heaven. He continued singing low with the singer, when a high-pitched noise disturbed him. He knew the noise was not from the song being played. He took a quick glance at his phone and found that someone was trying to call him. It was Viraj.

He picked it up.

"Hello?"

"Hi, bro"

"Yes, Viraj?"

"Do you have your phone with you now?"

"Then how do you think am I talking to you?"

"Oh right, look at the message I sent you"

Yugank tapped the phone several times until some pictures appeared. The pictures showed a boy in a thick forest. "Farhan is enjoying in a forest in foreign. And look at that tag, '#I am having an adventure'. Well, that triggered me" continued Viraj

"So what do you want me to do?"

"Don't you feel like being challenged?"

"Challenged? How?"

"I feel like Farhan thinks no one can go have an adventure like he does. Of course he does. That selfish boy! This is a clear challenge, Yugank. Let's go somewhere for an adventure and send the pictures to him directly."

"And what does that give you?"

"What does that give us? Satisfaction. Feel of Victory. A rebuff to his pride"

"Uh- I don't think that's needed."

"Why do you say that?"

"If the challenge you say isn't true, what will be left for us is embarrassment. I'm not in for it."

"Come on, Yuga! Think of it! You, me and the gang - somewhere in India, clicking selfies, having an adventure!"

"I don't think that'll work."

"All you need is time to think. Think and say yes or no, but don't choose the second option."

"I'll see"

"Bye. Think hard"

"Bye"

He took a deep breath and looked at the boy beside him. The boy was looking at Yugank with his big black eyes. He seemed like he heard the conversation between him and Viraj. The boy grinned and turned back. Yugank felt the embarrassment in the boy's mind.

"What is your name, kid?" he asked.

"Hruday" the boy replied.

"Looks like you're going home from school on your own. Which standard are you studying in?"

"Fifth"

"Aren't you scared of travelling in public buses, all alone?"

"To be honest, it is fun. Feels like an adventure." The boy said and left the bus at the stop it was in. Yugank sat still. 'Have an adventure' he thought, 'a kid is having an adventure. Hmm. Looks like I've thought hard'. He pulled his phone out again and started dialing Viraj.

CHAPTER II

Not Very Convincing Reason

Apoorva was alone at her house all-day, bored. She thought she had nothing to do. The last poem she had written made her feel she was an eternal being at last and her life was meaningful. She decided it to be the last poem she writes in her life.

She waited for her friends to come; at least then she can have someone to talk with. Then a thought struck her mind. She could write another poem referring to friends; especially them being late. She hopped to her chair and pulled it closer to the table before it. She held a pen in her palm and turned a page in her book. A minute passed by and nothing has changed, except for a word or two on the page. She had an end of her pen in her mouth, with her eyes staring at the roof.

Then someone knocked on the front door. It was Yugank.

"Oh, hi, Yugank. Come in" she said.

"No thank you, I am here to tell you something"

* * *

Daktar sat beside Shreni, his hair all messed up. He continuously kept nursing his palm which was on Shreni's hand. Daktar's palm had a wide strip of gradient red. He exhaled deeply. His head had confusion and anger over his professor, who had performed a rap on Daktar's hand that day.

Shreni gazed at the red strip, "Ah! That looks like it hurts a lot".

"How can he hit me with my own scale? Doesn't he have mercy over me for giving him the scale?" said Daktar, and with his other hand, set his hair back up.

Shreni shook her head in approval.

Daktar's phone rang. He had the ringtone which, no one else in the world has, but him. "It's Viraj" he said crossly, "He thinks I'm free now"

"Which you are" said Shreni, also crossly.

"Had you a rap on your hand, you would understand" replied Daktar and let the phone ring.

"At least cut the call, please. Your ringtone!" said Shreni, trying to bear it. And Daktar did so as said.

The sounds from the window seemed to change, suddenly. The loud grumbling sound of the auto had stopped now, and the air in their hairs had taken rest. They got off, and hanged their bags on their shoulders. Shreni paid the auto driver and they set to walk. That region of the town was not so crowded- which Shreni thought of as a great benefit. She didn't like to live congested. All she wanted in her life was an open area to live and of course, some money to spend.

They continued their walk into a narrow street, adjacent to the main road. Daktar's house was not very far from there, but Shreni's was. So he used to accompany her to her home and returned back to his. But just as they reached Daktar's house, a call from a familiar face above them made them stop there for a while. It was Yugank and Apoorva. They invited them upstairs, having already been there for ten minutes, to talk to them about something which needed decisions.

Half-an-hour passed and there came an agreement between the four, after a great debate. Daktar and Shreni had accepted for the trip, though Shreni was not totally convinced at the reason. They were told that the plans were to be discussed the next day at Daktar's house.

* * *

It was quarter-past noon, the next day, when they have assembled back at Daktar's house. It was the three of them again. Viraj and Mihira couldn't betray the function they were in. So they were called by phone. It was lifted on the other hand, and technically everyone was present at the venue. Yugank unlocked the silence.

"So, it was Viraj's idea though, that we are, perhaps, going to enjoy this weekend" said he.

"Then you have planned it for this weekend?" asked Shreni.

"Yes, I guess" Yugank replied.

"No, wait" started Viraj from the call, "First let's decide where we ought to visit. Later, the date"

"It was your idea of satisfaction or something. So you give the suggestions" Apoorva spoke to Viraj. Just then, a loud screeching noise of a trumpet sounded on Viraj's side.

"Viraj!" cried Shreni. The noise had high pitch. Then, sounds of running could be heard, as the sound faded. "Am I audible now?" said Viraj gasping.

"Yes. What was that, though?" asked Daktar, feeling peaceful.

"The function has begun. It was the noise of a trumpet" said Viraj,

"You start a discussion with a trumpet? What a grand and funny way to do that!" said Daktar, grinning. No one else laughed.

"Alright, we need to decide the location, right?"

"Yeah" said Shreni. There was a long pause of thinking on both the sides. Then she spoke, "How about a thick forest? The Kawwal Tiger Reserve. How does that sound?"

"Hmm... not exactly. We are not gonna copy him to visit a forest. If we do, everyone's gonna know that we did this, triggered by Farhan. Only then we would be embarrassed. Let's go somewhere else without forests" replied Viraj, "It would be better if the place was historic or geographically important"

There came a longer pause. "How about Trimbakeshwar? The source of Krishna" said Viraj.

"It's the source of river Godavari" corrected Shreni.

"Yes, something. How about that?" said Viraj. Another pause came.

"Won't there be forests there?" asked Daktar.

"Maybe, but it isn't exactly a forest where we are going, is it?" said Viraj, trying to convince them all, since he liked the importance of the place, and that it is unique and will satisfy his reason of going on a trip. The others had nothing to do but accept.

They soon took out their phones and ran an investigation about the trip's going and coming. The plans were soon made and the tickets were soon booked. They also decided what they had to take with them. It went beyond six o'clock in the evening until they were ready to pack the meeting up. Viraj tried to confirm if Mihira could come with them and was successful.

The plan, according to them, was simple. Daktar, Viraj, Apoorva and Shreni would board the train for Trimbakeshwar in the station of Devanagari. Whilst Viraj and Mihira had to attend the function they were having. So they won't be able to reach the station of Devanagari in time. They would board the train in that town of Shivadwar.

CHAPTER III

It Was The Crowd

The alarm echoed in the room with high-pitch. It had been a week since they've discussed the plans and the day of the trip has come. Daktar got up and fell back into the bed. Then he woke up again and found out that he only had one more hour to board the train! Then he blamed the alarm for his delay that it had only one job to do, and it failed. He tried to get ready as soon as possible that he missed a few calls from Shreni.

* * *

The Devanagari railway station was found to be very busy, since it was a festive holiday. Most of the travelers there were either visiting their families or going back home. Vendors were screaming, people were chattering, monkeys were resting over the roof of the platform, some of the people were chanting rhymes, some were carrying heavy bags, some were polishing shoes to earn a living, some were complaining to the station master, children were hopping around, babies were crying and the adults were trying their best to calm them down. The atmosphere was totally chaotic.

One of the samosa sellers on the platform, sad that no one had bought his products, walked around, searching for new people on the platform that he could sell his samosas to. He offered it to everyone the platform, until he came across Apoorva, who was standing on the platform. She, already bored, since no one has yet come, agreed to take one.

The samosa-man looked very desperate to earn from his samosas. Apoorva told to herself, that she, in some way, helped the man. His friends suspiciously moved around him as if they were spies. The seller sat on a bench and looked at one of his friends, who looked at him in return. The seller gestured to him as if he was complaining to him about his customers, and the friend twisted his lips and shook his head. Then the seller looked at the station hall, only to find new faces.

It was Yugank and Shreni. They had time saved in their watches and hence moved slowly across the platforms. Shreni had a good mood that day. She neatly combed her hair and her dress matched Yugank's. She hoped she could find a new experience from the trip. They descended on the busy platform no.2. Shreni was surprised by the crowd that day. How much crowd can stay in a platform at a time? Ten more people added to the platform results in people falling down on the tracks.

They were soon welcomed to the platform, by a short man in a t-shirt with a bag on his back.

"Welcome to the station, sir. My name is Guddu. You must be tired of travelling from home to here. Here, have a hot samosa and be refreshed" the man said. Yugank was impressed by the man, being addressed as 'sir'. So he tried to improvise.

"So you're selling samosas?" he said.

"Yes sir, the best ones. Look at these people" the old man said, pointing out to his friends, who started pretending like they were people who bought his samosas and started smiling, "they all loved them. Try one for yourself sir"

Shreni knew Yugank. She pulled back his hand from behind and whispered in his ear, "Don't, Yugank. It's unhealthy".

"Its fine" Yugank whispered back to her, "I'll handle this"

Then, Apoorva came out from nowhere and almost fell on Shreni. Shreni turned back furiously and was surprised to find Apoorva. "Why in the world would you push me like that!"

"It was the crowd" replied Apoorva. Soon, Yugank's conversation with the samosa-man attracted her attention.

Yugank looked at Apoorva and smiled. He accepted a samosa from the man and the man happily gave him it. Shreni knew she could do anything in the world but stop him. Yugank asked her if she wanted to have one too. She refused.

Few minutes passed by and Yugank felt uncomfortable inside him. He asked Shreni for a break and gave his phone to Apoorva to hold it for him until he comes. He headed for the station hall. Shreni smiled to herself. Yugank made his way over the tracks and onto the platform no.1. There he entered the station hall and advanced forward to the restrooms.

"I had one too. But I didn't feel that way" Apoorva said.

"That's Yugank there. He'll handle that" replied Shreni, grinning.

* * *

Daktar was standing off-limits with the support of the auto's seat. He wished the traffic jam would end sooner. He was stuck there for more than a minute now and was beginning to lose his patience. He quickly got off, paid the driver half the price and began to jog. He frequently kept asking to himself – why does this always happen to me? He couldn't jog faster with a heavy bag on his back.

He deeply looked at the texture of the pavement and half-ran. A moment later, he paused and looked back. There was the railway station. He walked backwards and into the station hall he went. He searched the second platform for familiar faces. Daktar hoped he reached the station on time. He was in the station hall when he found Shreni and Apoorva gazing at the railway tracks, standing on the second platform. Yugank wasn't with them.

Apoorva stood on the platform with Shreni and waited for Yugank. She just hoped he wouldn't be too late to board the train. Just as she thought, a voice came over a speaker in the platform – 'Attention! Train no. 203493; Mancherial Express is about to arrive at platform no. 2'. Both their hearts stopped. They looked longingly at the station hall but Yugank was nowhere to be seen. A shrill whistle from a long distance was heard. It was the train's!

From the announcement over thje speakers, Daktar could make out that the train was coming. 'Right on time' he thought. He immediately started running fiercely. He made his way through the people, into the first platform and to the over-bridge that connected both the platforms. Just as he skid on the first step, he felt the number of people on it doubled. 'Why now?'

* * *

Viraj had a bag in his hand and one on his back. Mihira trotted behind him. They walked slowly on the pavement towards the railway station. Viraj knew that the time was running slow for him at the moment. He wished that this wouldn't last long. Once they got into the train, time wouldn't stop for them. Hence, he was thinking of how to not let time slip out of his fingertips while he's at Trimbakeshwar.

The station came in no time.

They hadn't much to walk since the train was supposed to arrive at the first platform. They placed their bags by their legs, and sat down on one of the benches, Viraj panting. He had to carry two heavy bags, while Mihira carried a handbag; but yet, he hadn't complained. They sat there silently, watching the crowd move between platforms. The sky was cloudy with tiny gaps here and there. Viraj was extremely hoped the trip went well with no disturbance, for Daktar had fairly said he would punch him in the face if something goes wrong. He didn't want anything to happen then, unlike their last trip, when they happened to think of visiting their teacher who taught them at school but soon discovered on the day of travel, that their tickets were lost, thanks to Viraj.

He was blamed then. He was sure now that he has researched deeply about this trip but somewhere in his head was the insecurity of confirming the success of it.

Mihira thought the crowd was too much that day.

"I wonder why the crowd's much today" she screamed so that her brother could hear her through the noise of the station.

"There's some occasion in some village on the way to Nagpur. This crowd's for that, I guess. Let me ask one" Viraj shouted back and looked at the crowd. He held a man's wrist. The man looked at Viraj with irritation.

"Where is this crowd going?" Viraj shouted.

"Heera Ghat" shouted the man, "for tomorrow's festival!"

Viraj nodded and turned back but the man called him again.

"This is not the total crowd. You'll see a stampede when the train arrives!" he said.

"What train?" asked Viraj.

"Mancherial Express" said the man. Viraj nodded again and turned back to Mihira.

"Theirs' the same train as ours. We might find some discomfort when we board the train" he said. Mihira twisted her eyebrows and gazed round at the people before her. She wished they were all at their houses now, not making a mess at the station. But then she felt bad at herself for being so rude. Instead, she wished they were already at their destination; then both the parties could be happy.

CHAPTER IV

Diverging Footsteps

The magnificent sea-blue train slid on the tracks smoothly until it came to rest at Devanagari. Then it hooted loudly. Not many people pushed Shreni close to the train in their hurry to get on it. Apoorva was in absolute shock. She looked at the stairs connecting the over-bridge, wishing Yugank would suddenly appear on the platform and then they would get on. Yugank did not appear.

Shreni knew the train wouldn't wait any longer. So she went ahead into a car of the train. Apoorva tried to stop her. But Shreni stood on the footboard, looking at her and seeking with her eyes, for Yugank on the other side. Apoorva, at once had a feeling that she must urge Shreni to get down the train. A moment was all she had, to decide what to do. The Mancherial Express blew its whistle louder now, marking it's departure. Apoorva gasped, not understanding what to do. Soon enough, the cars rumbled and started moving. Shreni hurried Apoorva to get on the train, but she was just standing on the platform, stupefied.

Apoorva was in shock. The luggage was on the train with Shreni. It seemed Yugank was not coming. At first, she thought not to get on the train, but instead, wait for Yugank and see what they can do with the missing train. But then, she thought it would be better if she hopped on the train too, and so she did. She was standing in one of the last cars of the train; not at all in Shreni's. The train was moving. What have they done!

Recalling of what had happened, Shreni first blamed herself for getting on the train without Yugank and

Apoorva. Then she blamed Apoorva for not getting on the train when she called. After, she blamed Yugank for having that samosa. And again she blamed herself for not being so strict with the samosa-man. Then she gasped extremely loud and put her hand over her mouth. Daktar hasn't got into the train too! She hoped that at least Viraj would decide something to do.

In her hurry at the station, Apoorva had searched for a face of Yugank, but little did she know, that Daktar was running on the over-bridge, waving to her just when she decided to leap to the train. He descended on to the platform just when the train was in motion. He slid his palm over his head in frustration. He was confused over what had happened – why did Shreni get on the train even after she saw him waving to her? Where in the world was Yugank?

Just then, an announcement over the speakers caught his attention. 'Attention! Train no. 698237; Local Train is about to arrive at platform no. 4' it also said that its destination was Shivadwar.

He was then found sprinting on the over-bridge towards the platform on which the local train was about to arrive. He knew it was faster than regular trains, since it was made for covering little distance. He hoped if he took it he might reach Shivadwar by the time Mancherial Express gets ready for departure there. He hopped in, panting, and the train set out swiftly.

* * *

It was a while after Viraj spoke with the man, when a majority of the crowd moved towards the tracks. He thought, that might be the train coming.

"Come" he said to Mihira and with his bag hung to his shoulder, got up. Just at the moment when he was standing fully erect, a stampede, as the man had said, rushed into the station hall. It was about twice the already existing crowd. The people half-ran pushing everyone on their way. Viraj was thrown away from the bench and pushed towards the gathering at the tracks. One or two men in the front almost fell on the tracks with the velocity gifted by the new ones. They pushed everyone on the way. Viraj was amazed to see such crowd. They had no such thing as humanity or mercy, he thought.

Gradually, the hitting-each-other reduced, and they pressed each other close. Viraj could hardly breathe. He, with great effort, slithered through the crowd and moved backwards where he could sufficiently inhale. It was very chaotic with great amounts of people – hundreds of them, easily. Viraj felt for his bags – yes, he still had them. Then he looked around. Mihira was not with him!

"Mihira!" he shouted, seeking with his eyes, his precious sister. She was nowhere to be seen! 'She was probably pushed away by the crowd to the front' he thought. He couldn't let his sister struggle in the crowd. So he started moving through the crowd, to the front. He just wished he would find his sister safe before the train arrived, or it would become really hard for him. Just as he thought, a distant whistle was heard on the tracks.

* * *

Yugank felt comfortable then. He slowly walked out into the station hall, wondering why the crowd was suddenly less. He walked, sliding his feet on the smooth floor. Then he could see the platforms up ahead from where he stood. He looked for Shreni, who was not there.

He suddenly wrinkled his eyebrows and felt intense. He gazed once again, narrowing his eyes. Shreni wasn't there. Apoorva wasn't there too. For once, he would've thought they might've gone somewhere to buy some drink, maybe; but the absence of the luggage too made him feel insecure. It was clear that they were not on the platform. 'Let me see if I can find them in any of the shops here' he thought. He ran swiftly to the shops on platform no. 2. There were many of them, but it was easy to say that they were not there too, as there was not anyone in any of the shops. Where might they have gone?

Then something made him think of the train. Has the train already come? Did they get in it? Did he miss the train!? He fiercely ran to the information desk in the station hall. A young lady was there.

"Excuse me, miss" Yugank said politely.

"Yes? How can I help you?" the lady replied in the same way.

"Has the Mancherial Express arrived yet?" Yugank asked desperately.

"Arrived?" the lady chuckled, "It has departed too".

That's it. Yugank's cheerful cheeks dropped. How in the world did he miss the train!?

"Okay... What is the next local train to Shivadwar?" he asked, trying to be polite.

"In about five minutes" replied the lady, surprised by Yugank's sudden change of behavior. Yugank tightened his fists and groaned. He was to wait five more minutes! That wouldn't exactly give him the time to reach Shivadwar in-time.

CHAPTER V

Things Exit The Train

Apoorva was standing in horror. She was still stupefied. She could feebly feel the train pulling brakes gently. The train stopped. She looked out. It was the Nallapuram station, which was a small village between Shivadwar and Devanagari. She regretted for having entering the train at the last moment. 'However I need to find Shreni now if I stay' she thought and started searching for Shreni in the adjacent cars of the train. She couldn't enter into one of the cars, which was full of people. Apoorva blamed Shreni for not having a phone for herself. 'Instead, I can go back to Devanagari and tell Yugank what's happened' she thought, 'He'll be freaked out once he notices that we're not there or the train has gone. He might be waiting there for us too. If I can reach him in time, we can board the next train together'.

'Then why did I even board this train in the first place?' the other part of her brain asked, 'Pchh'. She stood there and thought in silence. She blamed Yugank for having given his phone to her; else, it would've been easier. Then she made her mind to go back for him.

She exited her car and stood on the platform. Then, she got reminded of Daktar. 'Gosh, this trip's a bummer!' she said to herself. She started running towards the station hall, to enquire for the next train to Devanagari.

Shreni was usually very patient, but now she wasn't. She was confused of what will happen then. She longed to reach the Shivadwar station sooner.

'Once I reach Shivadwar' she thought, 'I'll tell Viraj what had happened and then at least he would do something; call Yugank or Daktar. Gosh! I totally forgot about Daktar! He missed the train too! I hope at least he, Apoorva and Yugank will do something together. But... Daktar doesn't know where Yugank or Apoorva are! Blow!'

She looked out of her window and noticed Apoorva running. She was on the train after all! Shreni tried to call her, but in vain. She screamed for Apoorva but she just couldn't hear her. She couldn't get off as the train started moving again.

Shivadwar was reached in no time. Just as the train slowed down, heaps of people shot down on the car. The pressure of getting in was so high and hence, no one could get out. No one wanted to, though, except Shreni. She moved further back. She was half-afraid that the train shall start moving before she got out. The people blocked every single door and window. It was dark in the car. The crowd kept falling on each other, trying to get on the train. There were all kinds of people – old people, young ones, some about sixty, men, women, including children. There was nowhere to move, except to dance with every wave of pushing by the people in the front. Shreni urgently wanted to get out of the train, but nobody let her. The murmurs of the people and cries of their children entered into her ears like the roar of a giant waterfall. She could bear it no more. Exhausted and angry, both on the people and Viraj, she thought she wouldn't get out that day if she just stayed there. So once the number of people coming inside reduced, she started screaming and pushed everyone to the entrance of the car. She pushed several teens and one of them caught her hand instead. She looked back, red. It was Mihira! She looked all tired and a feeble smile was on her face. She held Mihira tightly. She looked around for Viraj, thinking he would be there, holding Mihira's hand but Gosh! He was nowhere about.

"Where's Viraj?" Shreni cried.

"I don't know! I lost him!" Mihira cried back.

'He might still be outside' Shreni thought.

"Move! Everyone!" she shouted at the top of her voice and advanced forward, dragging Mihira with her. Some kind people on the way, moved, but some didn't. Shreni pushed everyone until she could see the door. Her luggage, including Mihira was slowing her down, being an additional weight and an additional volume.

The train then hooted. Shreni's heart stopped. She then put the humanity in the farthest corner of her mind and using all her strength, fiercely made her way to the door. The train hooted again, and the car's floor below them rumbled. The train was to move in a moment, when Shreni tackled the last person, who was standing on the footboard, and made it to the platform at last. She threw her bags on a bench and sat down, catching her breath. Before her and Mihira, the train slowly moved out of the station.

Mihira thought Shreni was out of her mind. "Why would you pull us out of the train?" said the confused girl.

Shreni didn't speak. "There's no one in the train" she said after a while, gasping for air.

"What?"

Shreni had a tough time explaining her what had happened, in the shortest way possible. But then she remembered Viraj again. "Where is Viraj?" she asked in hurry.

"I don't know" Mihira said and it was her chance now, to narrate her story. Shreni went blank. Viraj surely didn't board the train... or did he?! Some corner of her mind told her that there were chances that Viraj hadn't boarded the train, looking for his lost sister, and instead, stayed on the platform. He loved his sister of course. He wouldn't just leave her. So they decided to search for Viraj; if he surely is there.

* * *

Apoorva hadn't reached the enquiry centre yet, when an announcement came over the speakers, making it clear that the local train which was on the second platform, was to set out for Devanagari. Apoorva didn't think twice. She ran to the second platform and boarded the train just when it started moving.

* * *

Wind hit Daktar's tuft on his forehead and it swung back. He utterly cursed his alarm clock, for he thought it was the reason he missed the train. He felt he was in too much hurry to sit in a seat; and so he stood at the door of a car in the local train. He was really confused. 'Yugank and Shreni might have already got into the train' he thought, since he has not seen them anywhere near Apoorva.

'How dare they?' he said to himself, 'Yugank knew I was coming; Apoorva saw me coming; and yet, they did not wait for me! Just wait till I reach the train at Shivadwar. Yugank's gonna die today'

Then he got reminded of Viraj. 'Once Mancherial Express arrived at Shivadwar, Viraj and Mihira would get in and wonder why I am not with Yugank. Then they might wait for me' Daktar wished his train reached Shivadwar before the Express's departure, 'What if they lose hope that I'm coming? Its better if I call Viraj now'. He dragged his phone out of his shirt pocket and started dialing Viraj. Viraj, on the other hand, did not answer.

23

Just then, the train Daktar was in, stopped at a little station. Daktar hung up the call and tried once again. Yet, no answer; instead, it said Viraj's phone was out of network coverage area. Daktar groaned.

The train started moving again. It was not out of the station yet, when Daktar was standing on an edge of the door, holding his phone freely. Daktar's car moved to one of the pillars at a corner of the tracks and it struck the phone in his hand. Daktar could not get hold of it as soon as it got knocked out of his hands. The phone fell dramatically on the platform. He could do nothing but stare at it. A board stating 'Nallapuram' passed by and soon the railway station was out of sight.

Daktar then came into his consciousness and he cursed himself for holding his phone so recklessly; now he has lost his only hope in contacting the others.

CHAPTER VI

Broken Screen

Shreni and Mihira soon found that they could find no Viraj. There was still a good amount of crowd on the platform. Shreni felt lost for a moment or two. Could Viraj have really boarded the train? She put her palm on her forehead and sat down on a bench. She began to feel if that yellow-shirt-guy who pushed her in the train was him. He did not know no one was in the train!

Shreni and Mihira sat in silence for a moment. Then Mihira recalled of having told by Shreni that Apoorva was seen in the Nallapuram station.

"You told you saw Apoorva in Nallapuram?" she asked Shreni. Her face brightened with hope.

She could see a local train on the platform, arriving just then. Shreni caught an old lady's wrist and asked if that train was supposed to go to Nallapuram next. The old lady nodded. That was the only thing Shreni wanted. She hopped into the train with Mihira in her hand.

They, in their hurry, missed a really needed help; Daktar was just coming out of the same train from the car beside theirs. He rushed out of the train and looked around. He called an old woman and asked if the Mancherial Express had left.

The old woman, muttering "Why does everyone keep asking me things today?" did not answer. He had no time to waste. He ran to the enquiry centre and asked for the Mancherial Express. A moment later, his face turned white and red at the same time. He screamed at himself. 'Viraj and Mihira might have got into the train. Why did they not do something for me? Maybe at least try and call me!' Then he remembered where his phone actually was.

His dropped eyes thought he caught a sight of Mihira in the exact train in which he reached there. He twisted his eyebrows and rubbed his eyes to see more clearly. It was Mihira with Shreni indeed! He ran fast, shouting her name. Neither Mihira, nor Shreni noticed Daktar yelling. Daktar was halfway from the enquiry centre, when the train hooted and moved out of the station.

* * *

Yugank kept saying to himself that he will not be able to reach Shivadwar in time. He looked at his watch. More than seven minutes passed by since when he asked the lady at the enquiry centre. An announcement was heard over the speakers and the local train he was waiting for, has come. He ran into one of the cars. Little did he know that Apoorva was on the same train!

She sprinted out from the other car and started looking around for Yugank. She couldn't see him on the platform. The train behind her, set off again. Apoorva ran through the over-bridge and onto the first platform.

'Yugank might not have come from where he went the last time' she thought, 'Ugh. How long does he take?' Despite her hurry, she had to wait in the station hall, impatiently. She, in the next second, took her phone out and called Yugank. It rang in her pocket. 'Why did he even give his phone to me?' Then she remembered Daktar and called him. The call was not answered.

* * *

Shreni and Mihira were in Nallapuram in no time. The station contained a remarkable amount of people. They looked everywhere.

"Mihira" Shreni said after a moment, "You search for Apoorva in the second platform; I will search for her in the station hall and the first platform; and we meet again, after exactly five minutes and exactly here"

"What if we get lost again?" Mihira asked.

"We won't. Don't you have a phone?" asked Shreni crossly.

"I don't" replied Mihira sarcastically, "Do you?"

Shreni looked at her for a moment, her eyes narrowed. "Fine" she said, "Let us both look for her together"

They searched across platforms for Apoorva. They couldn't find her there. 'I saw her here' thought Shreni, 'She must be here somewhere!'

They searched everywhere, to every end of the platforms. Finally, they stopped at an end of the first platform. They couldn't find Apoorva near the shops, in the station hall or in any of the platforms. Shreni was working in her mind, the plan of what she must do then. All of a sudden, a familiar sound came out of nowhere. It was that awful ringtone of Daktar's phone. Shreni looked everywhere about and found the phone before a pillar, at her feet. She picked it up. The phone was the one that made the sound. The screen of the phone was broken. 'It's Daktar's!' Shreni said, 'Why in the world would it be here?'

The sound came from the phone again. Apoorva was calling. Shreni immediately picked it up with hope.

"Daktar!" said Apoorva, panting, "I've been calling you for ages!"

"Apoorva, this is Shreni. Where are you? I came to Nallapuram to find you but you're not here!"

"Why are you in Nallapuram? And... you aren't in Mancherial Express? And... Daktar's with you?" asked Apoorva, surprised.

"I came here to find you! And... no; And... no again. I found his phone here"

"Why in the world would it be there?"

"I don't know. Daktar might have already reached Shivadwar. Where are you though?"

"I've come back to Devanagari for Yugank. Come meet me here in the station hall!" Apoorva noticed her phone having really low battery, "Quick! My phone's going to be dead!"

The call got cut.

"What did she say?" Mihira asked. Shreni's face glowed with hope, once again. She told Mihira that Apoorva was waiting for them in Devanagari. In their excitement of finding Apoorva soon, they took the train that was on the first platform. they stood freely, in the car having less crowd. The doors of the car were closed and the floor below them rumbled. The train hooted. It just set to move when Mihira, who was looking at the window, touched Shreni arm, her smile turning flat. Shreni asked her what was wrong. Mihira pointed out to the platform. Shreni looked out of the window too.

"People?" she said. Mihira shook her head.

Electric poles appeared after the train quit the station.

"Poles?" Shreni asked.

Mihira said coldly after a while, "Those poles are supposed to go right if this train's going to Devanagari". Shreni looked closely. The electric poles moved left. "Did you even enquire where this train was going?"

CHAPTER VII

Finding Whereabouts

Yugank was irritated of what happened. His train stopped at Nallapuram station for a while. He stood still, not uttering a word.

'There is no way we will reach the station with the Mancherial Express still there' he thought, 'NO WAY.' Poor Yugank; little did he know that if at least he had shouted that out loudly, the two girls in the car beside his' would rush up to him. Yugank looked out of the window, expecting Shivadwar station to appear sooner. He could see several electric poles, moving left from the right part of the window railing.

***

Viraj, tired of searching for his sister, decided that she might have boarded the Mancherial Express. He did not know what to do. He tried calling the others several hundred times, but one was busy, one was busier and the other was busiest. He wanted to tell them that Mihira was on the train too with them.

A minute later, he lost hope in calling the others too. 'They might be busy handling the crowd that entered the train' he thought. He sat before one of the shops on the first platform. He knew Daktar would kill him if he came to know. Then he blamed himself for including his sister into the group.

***

Daktar was in a way, shocked and in a way, sad too. 'So Shreni and Mihira didn't board the train' he thought, 'Why in the world would they not?'

Then an announcement came over the speakers stating a local train to Devanagari. Daktar stood and thought, 'Shreni and Mihira would've definitely gone to Devanagari; in search of me, maybe? However, if I'd get a clue of what had happened, this would be the only way I'd get it'. Thinking so, he hopped on to the train to Devanagari. God knows what he was doing.

* * *

Apoorva was the most worrying one; she thought. She was impatient and she accepted that. Sitting in the station hall and waiting was the worst job for anyone; she decided. She could neither wait a little more for a person who took a break for more than two hours now, which started to seem unnatural, or just stay there as she believed Shreni would be coming to save her from that, nor could she go somewhere, in search of Yugank or Daktar maybe, as she trusted that Shreni was coming. She took her phone out again and was utterly disappointed when she saw it was dead.

More than half of her heart seemed to vote to stand and go in search of someone. And she did so.

Apoorva wandered in the station hall and on the platform no. 1. A train arrived. She hoped Shreni was in it, and so she rushed back to the station hall and got seated. A minute passed by, but no one came to meet her. Apoorva was disappointed. Then, a mysterious chuckle was heard from behind her. A teen boy with a shallow beard, who was behind her, chuckled again and put his hand over her shoulder. Apoorva turned back in distress, which turned into anger as soon as she saw that it was Daktar.

"You were here the whole time?" she shouted in anger.

"No, I took a train to Shivadwar after missing the Mancherial Express" said Daktar, "Then, at Shivadwar, I saw Mihira and Shreni come here. So I decided to come here too”

"Mihira's with Shreni?" Apoorva asked.

"Yes" replied Daktar.

There was a moment of silence.

"But Shreni hasn't arrived yet!"

* * *

The train Yugank was in reached Shivadwar.

He rushed out and looked around. People were everywhere. An old woman walked before him. He called out to her and asked her if the Mancherial Express had left. The old woman looked at Yugank angrily and impatiently. She cursed him in herself and resumed walking.

'No use' thought Yugank and immediately sprinted to the enquiry centre. The lady at the enquiry desk looked at Yugank, just like the old woman had looked, but as half of hers. Yugank was confused and told to himself that the people now-a-days have no respect to give. The enquiry lady shook her head to his question. Yugank was tired, angry, confused, and what not. He had lost all hope. He imagined in his mind, the hopefulness of Shreni, the irritation of Daktar, the excitement of Mihira, the tension of Viraj and the thinking of Apoorva, as they all sit in the Mancherial Express, not at all bothering about Yugank. He then blamed the samosa-man, "This is all his fault. What was his name? Ugh!... who cares?"

He walked slowly and reluctantly towards the station hall, where he saw a row of shops. 'A cool drink would do for a defeat' he said to himself and walked towards a shop having a fridge on the outside. Just as he reached it, he could see a couple of closed shutters, before one of which, was perched Viraj.

* * *

Shreni and Mihira got off at Shivadwar.

"However we are going to go to Shivadwar, and we know Daktar might be there. So we could search for him and find him by chance, and then take a train to Devanagari for Apoorva" they had discussed in the train.

Just as they discussed, they started searching for Daktar, platform to platform.

"You have Daktar's phone, right?" Mihira asked Shreni.

"Yes" Shreni replied.

"Why don't you try to call the other then?" Mihira asked.

"I tried. The screen's broken. It isn't touch-sensitive anymore" Shreni replied, sadly.

They had searched for more than a minute and were tired.

"I think Daktar has boarded the Mancherial Express" said Mihira, "Do let's stop now and initiate the remaining part of the plan"

"Yes, let's wait for the next train to Devanagari"

* * *

Yugank and Viraj were standing on the first platform of the Shivadwar station. Viraj had his phone in his hand and his finger was dancing on its screen. Then he lifted it up to his ear. Shreni picked his call up on the other hand.

"Houston, we have a problem!" Viraj said, "We couldn't board the train"

"We have one too" replied Shreni on the other hand.

"Shreni? Where are you?" asked Viraj.

"Not at all in the Mancherial Express" Shreni replied.

Viraj was in shock. He held the phone away from his ear and told Yugank that Shreni was not in the Mancherial Express. Then he put the phone back to his ear.

"Where are you now then?"

"I am currently in a train, going to Devanagari. Mihira's with me too" Shreni replied, "Haven't you boarded the train?"

"No, we haven't. Yugank's with me. Thank god you have Mihira. I was worried about her"

"Where are you?"

"At Shivadwar"

"What? We searched the whole station but haven't found you guys!"

"We are on the platform no. 1 now"

"Don't care. Come and meet us in the Devanagari station. Apoorva told me that she would be there"

"Alright. Will be there soon"

CHAPTER VIII

Apoorva In Black

Itfelt unnatural for Apoorva and Daktar to just stay there for hours, with no purpose. Shreni was supposed to come way before Daktar, if she was really coming when Daktar saw her the last time.

"I'm sure they were coming here" said Daktar.

"But I don't see them now" replied Apoorva crossly.

They soon started to feel doubtful on Shreni's arrival. They hadn't much to debate on, to decide to go back to Shivadwar, in case they could find her and Mihira, as they were both waiting to propose the idea. It was just matter of minutes until Daktar and Apoorva were in one of the local trains to Shivadwar, which was on the first platform. The train set out swiftly. Daktar told Apoorva not to rethink of the decision made; it would just result in regret.

They stood close to the footboard of their car. Half of the journey was made, when there came a loud rumbling and screeching noise from the front of the train. It shook all the cars. Daktar almost fell out of the train. Then the train's velocity reduced slowly, until the train was stopped at last, several meters away from the Nallapuram station. They wondered why the train would stop there.

After a while, a bald and short man, walking along the length of the train, shouted, "Passengers must get down here and walk to the station!"

Daktar got down, followed by Apoorva. He called the short man.

"Excuse me, what has happened?" he asked.

"The train's engine broke down, sir. We're sorry but you must walk to the station" the man replied.

"Oh, just the thing we needed!" said Apoorva, irritated to her toe.

"What? How can a train break down?" Daktar asked, surprised.

"I'm sorry but it did, sir" replied the man.

They had nothing to do but to walk to the Nallapuram station along with the fellow passengers. Daktar muttered and Apoorva mumbled, as they walked to the station. There was an announcement, repeatedly running over the speakers, "Attention! Local Train no. 493173 has been removed from the schedule due to engine issue. Do not panic. Another train shall be arranged for you"

Apoorva and Daktar stood in silence. 'JUST WHY WOULD THIS HAPPEN NOW?'

"I think we shall neither reach Shivadwar anytime soon, nor can anyone find us here" said Apoorva, "Why did we not wait in Devanagari?"

* * *

Yugank and Viraj stood in a train which was moving towards Devanagari. Yugank was happy that they were going to meet at last; and Viraj was happy that he was going to find Mihira.

Yugank kept reciting that they were supposed to meet Shreni and Mihira in the station hall; as he would not trust Viraj for anything like that. He looked out of the window. Green crop fields expanded to infinity. Suddenly, an announcement came over the speakers of the train that it would not stop at Nallapuram. Everything was finally coming together. Several poles appeared beyond the window and then, the station of Nallapuram was seen.

Viraj saw groups of people on the first platform and then, a train was visible on the tracks. Viraj's smile flattened. He poked Yugank on the shoulder.

"Yes?"

"Was that Apoorva on the first platform?" asked Viraj, doubtfully.

"What?"

"Was that Apoorva in black?"

"In the station?"

"Yes"

"How can she be in Nallapuram?" Yugank twisted his eyebrows.

"I don't know. I feel like I saw her" said Viraj.

"Are you sure?"

"Not exactly" said Viraj coming out of the gloom. He thought for a moment, "No, it can't be her"

* * *

It was the one moment in the whole day that Shreni thanked Viraj for something. If he hadn't called her, he and Yugank would've been still lost.

The train reached Devanagari. Shreni and Mihira got down, as the powerful sun beamed down on them. They ran to the first platform and into the station hall. They looked around. Most of the chairs there were unseated; and certainly, Apoorva was not in the people who were seated. They started getting tensed again. They ran all over the station but haven't found Apoorva anywhere. Where could she be?

A train hooted in the first platform and Viraj and Yugank got out of it. They were received by Shreni and Mihira with a hug.

"Where's Daktar?" asked Yugank.

"We've searched for them, but they aren't anywhere"

"What?!"

"Are you sure you've searched the whole station?"

"We did"

They stood on the platform and thought for a moment. After a while, Viraj whispered to Yugank, "Do you think the one I saw in Nallapuram station was indeed Apoorva?"

Yugank yelled, "Oh! Yes! Yes, it might be Apoorva!"

"What happened?" Mihira asked. The girls were soon told of what happened in the train at Nallapuram. Enquiry was soon made, and the train to Nallapuram, which they were waiting for, arrived like a grand chariot.

* * *

The passengers were sent to the second platform, and among them were Apoorva and Daktar. They could be described as the most impatient among all of them. Several trains came and went. About fifteen minutes passed by, and a newly arranged train was ready on the tracks. The crowd was sucked in through the doors of the cars. Daktar was deciding whether to or not to enter the train. Then, he decided to. He walked towards one of the cars of the train. Apoorva entered the train and Daktar was about to step into it when he was caught by the collar and pulled out. It was the gang.

"You were here the whole time, Daktar?" asked Shreni.

Apoorva was still on the train as the train started moving. She immediately hopped down before the train sped off.

They were surprised to see each other gathered again. All of them burst into a thundering of words as they met.

"Where were you guys?"

"Guess you never wanted to find me so bad?"

"Where did you find Mihira?"

"You missed the train too?"

"I thought you would hit him hard, Daktar?"

"Already did"

"Daktar, here's your phone. I found it on the platform, here"

"Oh thank you, Shreni. I thought I lost it"

"You did"

"Here, Yugank, take your phone. And never give it to me again"

Everyone was tired, and they sat comfortably on a bench.

"Enough of the adventure, Viraj? Satisfaction? Feel of victory?"

"I do feel like we won, though"

www.ingramcontent.com/pod-product-compliance
Lightning Source LLC
Chambersburg PA
CBHW030506170726
47990CB00008BA/3065